VillainElle

Also by Lynn Crosbie

Miss Pamela's Mercy

The Girl Wants To

VillainElle

Lynn Crosbie

Coach House Press
Toronto

Coach House Press
50 Prince Arthur Avenue, Suite 107
Toronto, Canada
M5R 1B5

First Edition
Printed in Canada

Published with the assistance of the Canada Council, the Ontario Arts
Council, the Ontario Publishing Centre and the Department of Canadian
Heritage

Canadian Cataloguing in Publication Data
Crosbie, Lynn, 1963 —

VillainElle
Poems.
ISBN 0-88910-470-0
I. Title.

PS8555.R61166V5 1994   C811'.54   C94-930320-8
PR9199.3.C76V5   1994

For Tony

The Super Nevada: Carol, Patti, Marjorie, Lisa-Jane, Janet,
Barb, Mary-Jo, Leslie, and Mary: The Low Rider

and in memory of Daniel Jones

I'd like to thank the following people for their support,
advice and encouragement:

Tony Burgess, Patti Seaman, Joanne Balles, Carol Dalziel,
Mary Nyquist, David Trinidad, Kevin Connolly, Jeffery
Conway, David McGimpsey, Alice Palumbo, Rex Kay, Sam
Rosenbaum, Daniel Jones, Clint Burnham, Nancy Johnston,
Fred Flahiff, Leslie Sanders, Thom Jurek, Casey Hermansson,
Suzy Richter, the *Motorcycle Betrayers* (for divine
inspiration), Chris Dewdney and the Coach House staff.

Thanks too to the Toronto and Ontario Arts Councils for
their assistance and belief in this project.

Finally, I would like to thank my family.

Many of these poems have appeared in *What!, Alphabet City,
Shift, Room of One's Own, Quarry, Apostle's Bar, Pan del
Muerto, Fireweed, Hart House Review, Crash, Errata,* and
Who Torched Rancho Diablo?, and several were collected in
I Eat Your Flesh (Streetcar Editions, 1993).

Believe me, I knew you, though faintly, and I loved, I loved you
All.

Gwendolyn Brooks

ᔧ All About Eve

I don't know just where I'm going
but I'm going to try for the kingdom if I can
      —The Velvet Underground

each time I see her, in *Harper's Bazaar* or *Vogue,*
I tear another pink iris, orange freesia,
from the Chelsea wallpaper. and I stand
on the black metal balcony and sing, Madame
Butterfly. I wish I was the poison in
your heart, Eve. I see it cluster, a
wasp-yellow fury, the lines of the
pillbox hat, the ribbon-cape, the
figure-eight skirt you stole from me.
my glory is ash and bone beneath my
brilliant fingers, and the silkworm
expends her yellow labours for you.
Eve would bring me orchids in terra-
cotta pots. I named the bulbs in the
baked earth, she said, I watched the
sun begin and saw your face in the water.
your four-leaf clover gown was the birth
of the Nile. she makes pious designs,
O gloriose Virgem e Martir, white linen
sheaths, a bracelet of half-moons and arrowheads.
she draws baby's breath on the hems of her
dresses, she believes that Jesus is her
couturier. He made this golden cloth from
lambswool, His wounds are the wine velvet
seams and lining. she pencils in my eyebrows,
a radiant arch, the *M* dark blue against
my pallor. she is still at the mirror,

holding my scissors like a metal
angel. I want to plunge them,
deep between her ribs where the sixes meet,
in nightshade and sulphur. my designs are
original, my Athena. I watched them
jealously, on the thighs and shoulders
of beautiful men. I could be vicious if
she crossed me, that mark in the cavalry
of her scalp, I sent her a hatbox of moths,
I danced in the streets in her ivory slippers.
the weeds and dust on the soles, is art,
I told her. you could frame my straight-pins
and thimble with the *Primavera,* my work-
table is a Venetian altar. I sleep in
the sunlight, dreaming sweetbriar collars and
nightingales. Eve, I would say on this
honeymoon, her mouth a devotion, I want
to go downtown. please baste that moiré
slip and bring me a tenth, a point of light.
my heroine, she kissed the veins of my
wrists and ankles, she combed me with a diamond
syringe. and the opium bled in flowers from
the glass, each perfect carat blooming in
my heart. I watched her scrape her name,
a palimpsest, over mine. she said she
loved me, my neck is passion-violet under
the bruises. I see all of creation in her
pockets and handbag, a spool of thread tangled
in her heels, her radiant fame. my life is
intolerable without her, she pieces my
flesh into each of her designs.
my room is a Troy of plates and eggshells,
that splinter beneath my feet.

here in the narrow chamber, I hear the
absence of my desire, choral despair.
my arms are vivid spirographs, folded poppies.
I stab each ellipse in the centre, I am
the rightful queen. her prayer is
pressed to my immortal soul when I
fall before my religion, beauty,
and forgive her. *in death there is no remembrance*,
and though I walk in the valley of its shadow,
I am not afraid.

✺ Saturday Night Fever

I'm going nowhere
*   somebody help me*
*   somebody help me there*

His white suit a peerless lily the wide lapels
an allegorical breastplate. the *Prima Porta Augustus*,
his arm-divine is raised to the glittering ceiling.
            I am the little cupid that clings to
                    his thigh—symbolizing Venus, Venus
Goddess of love that I am. when he holds me and we dance,
    my cool silk dress skims my thighs, arouses me and I am
more than a woman,
                        more than a woman when I defile his neck,
his spotless collar with coral—the pink/orange skeleton:
my lips are jewellery. but as my body pushes closer,
the membrane (the colony) of my desire, he moves, elegantly,
easily, from me

there are two kinds of girls—and nice girls don't—
        push him into the car   Bobby C and Double J
dangerous, circling outside. his gold chains are hot on
            my breastbone—
white bliss when he pushes my skirt higher, higher—*heaven*,
and stops: *just give me a blow job.*

that night I experienced love, not love. wanting
all of him, he looks away, wanting more. the Brooklyn Bridge,

a temple-icon at his throat. I see his dreams are hopeless,
small. and still, I follow him. to the hardware store, and finger

nails screws rakes. I want him to brush my body with Plaster of Paris,
cool enamel paint, until I am pale, bridal, the tender moon.

to show him that there are *sublunary lovers*, that there is
nothing between his fine chalk suits, his blue work smock:

mutability and constancy: there are spheres, turning endlessly
in the skies. where angels sing in *a harmony of ravishing beauty*.

I decide to sleep with him instead. there is a selection of
        condoms in my hand when I reach for him
outside the 2001. the science-fiction of the evening;
        he slaps them to the ground, as if I am alien,
clinical, devouring. and walks, incurious of longing,
        space.

Joey is pacing the sidewalk, in perilous platforms, crying
call me Tony, call me—are you going to call me Tony?

I am plotting revenge, a night of abandon, near
oblivion, I do not recognize him, my subjectivity—
doubled

envying his power, despising his weakness

(that) car is idling, when Tony approaches. his face is
        battered, still lovely, his life is changing: this night,
I drink moonshine from a flask and lay down between his
        friends as we drive. strange tongues, teeth assail me,
he asks: *are you happy, are you happy now?* his disgust
        is a tonic

I close my eyes at the whiteness the
glare of their exposed underwear, I imagine

they are vulnerable, that I dictate their
yearning: *how deep is your love*, your love

I thought I wouldn't cry, it felt like something,
something better than

loneliness, anguish: Joey is climbing the golden spires
of the bridge

exultant and desperate. he is showing them, he is showing me
that there are times

when your chest splits and separates and there is your heart.
broken, beating, there are such terrible miracles

his body demolished beneath the water, my screams
exalting him.

I let them lead me away, because they are afraid. but it is this:
the sweet descent of his dauntless body, the
healing black water, a dark coronet

that bears him below and carries him, it carries me to safety.

∽ VillainElle

for Aileen Wuornos

Come now, do this, my soul! No secret murder
earns renown; proclaim in people's eyes
your cruel and bloody skill.
  —Medea

I painted a picture for Arlene, and wrote
across the moon and stars, *pick a dream /*
any dream. longing here, for her
consultant fingers, an arcana of cards
splayed over my desolate body.
empêchement, déplaisir, une lettre,
une brune, la mort. she says she
wishes she was a magician; she would
get me out of here, keys sewed in her
palms, she would pull silver from my
ears, my mouth. she is my last chance,
I asked her to help me, *I need to change*
before I fall. I have killed seven men.
each time, I flagged them down and *I put them*
out of their misery. I would stand by the
topless bar, by the highway and smile and say,
hello handsome. hello baby, could I get
a lift? and kiss them, empty their pockets
and strip off their clothes. take it all off,
I said, and shot them dead. Arlene, I wrote,
you are way too kind / to get to know my kind
of mind. but if you listen, I will tell you
where it ended and I began.

Was there another Troy for her to burn?

seven marks on the wall, seven shadows.
I know that I left Troy, Michigan,
behind me. but the men I grew up
with interface, brother stepfather
grandfather. my corner of the yellow house
was draped in pink chenille, a daisy
clock, a baby doll that cried and cried.
they would circle my bed, and I buried myself
under the sheets, percale smooth, frayed
from my teeth, my screams! suddenly, they,
he pushed my hands behind my back and covered
my mouth. I can't remember, the grass, the daisies
leave orange silt on my legs and the sky is
black. the sky, my mother, is a cold
compress and his tongue his pores his eyes
are not there. nothing, but the pain and
that never goes away, *I have to stop the
pain.* his low growl, the hair raised on
his neck, his brilliant teeth. they travel in
packs, picking her bones, fleece, muscle,
she is lost and far from home and when she hears
them in the wind she is afraid.
I turned mean back then. *listen you old
bastard if you ever touch me again, I'll
tear you to pieces and eat your flesh.* I
imagine a bloody trail, ear eyelid thigh
foot that leads to the seashore. taking
his magic, my magic and I leave, with a dragon at
my heels and their voices, calling.

In Florida the living is easy. I pull on
my stockings dress and stiletto heels; I
stand on the corners, where the palm trees

are. their serrated leaves fringe your
picture Arlene, and lizards hang on the
windowpanes, I said, do you feel lonely,
or would you like some company? but it
wasn't the work, it was their faces,
destitute and barren. without her,
I would have killed them sooner, *earthly*
words cannot describe how I felt about
her. beautiful Tyria, I cherish the night we
met at the Last Resort when she nailed my slip
to the bar and we danced until we were breathless.
why don't you do something, she said, if you
can't stand it any more. my hate was palpable,
something between us. I know you can't understand,
but the first time, seeing him crumpled beside me,
I just fell in love.

I became careless and they found me. they combed my
apartment and found glass cleaner, bullets,
tattered neckties, but I never surrendered.
and so, you found me here, in the last place
I'll ever live, in these pious chambers.
you touch me through the mesh and bars, and
wonder at the danger. does your skin burn,
on contact? I think you are enamoured of
my history, you wear my death like pendant
earrings and never ask, I lived in the forest
once, when I ran away. and dreamed below the
poplars, in the ferns and moss. it is there that
I perfected my *cruel and bloody skill*, and it
is here I am devoted to the memory. you want
to save me, so I'm asking you. to slip in at
night and take my clothes. the shapeless grey dress,

the embroidered numbers. to cover your face,
and I will leave, as you, and drive away. you can
hope and pray, as they strap you into the electric
chair, but I will be gone. long gone, as the
smoke plumes from your temples and your eyes bake
under their metal vices. I will be cruising,
slowly along the highway, smiling at your grief,
your error. I never cared, Arlene, and I never will;
I'm strange that way.

☜ Betty and Veronica

an image is a state of the soul
between women
a state of the soul is an image
  —Nicole Brossard

today was a day like any other,
I stayed in my room and burned incense—
love me fairy cones—and dreamed
about Veronica. I saw her black hair,
its streaks—*lapis lazuli*—in the
crown of ash. I thought jealously
of her small hands in his, of the
squash-coloured stains at the nape
of her neck. where his cold lips embellished
her beauty, his ankles are pale beneath the
vine. the abrasions are cactus flowers,
scorpions, these shapes corrupt her memory.
I saw her when she kneeled beside him and
held her veil against him and Veronica

irons her religion to her sleeves and pockets,
his sorrowful face is golden, luminous,
a decal on each *ensemble*. she laminates
every tear with clear nail polish and
tells me I know nothing about love.
she says these are *the days of vengeance*,
and she is suspended, when she throws stones
through the classroom windows. I want to
kiss her, I am desperate, but she denies
me this betrayal. I am reduced to staring
at my idol, when she passes me in the

streets. once, I saw her at a perfume counter,
spraying her wrists with an atomizer of
Shalimar. her serene eyes were clouded with
mystery and that night I left lilies on
her doorstep. her delicate feet are
a garland of flowers, a string of pearls
in platform sandals, an altar

I pin my prayers to a photograph of her,
she is burning money and her arms are
spread open, she is bleached by the
light of the sun. and I pray, she will
come to me tonight and bless my body
with her hot breath and cruel mouth.
I am lost inside of her, as her spirit
becomes flesh, generous and sweet.
I hear her walking in the grass, circling
the garden below. she calls to me,
to join her and she tells me how she
hates me. his impression, soulful,
cryptic, rejects me too but I
reach for her, still, for her
faithless heart and we fall to the
earth, struggling, and wild with
desire.

ᔄ I Eat Your Flesh

But I have done a thousand dreadful things
    —Titus Andronicus

1

I knew I loved him long before he treated me,
in the saltwater, cold moonshine of his office.
where anemones bloom in pale red plankton and I lay
down in the darkness and coral. his eyes were calico
scallops, lettered olive, lime star shells; I have
done a thousand dreadful things since then. I
have planted stakes in his grave to protect him;
his lost voice was the sigh, the breath of an oyster.
I pressed metal buddhas, crosses, hexagrams into his soft
skin, and made a chain of cultured pearls. he fell into me,
and couldn't breathe, he sent circles, signs to the
surface. danger, in the black and blue sea that
bruises the shore, in the architecture of the moon.
time moved slowly when we were together, a
galaxy of particles, a heterotic strand. I would
stare at his rings, and imagine we were sealed
in their orbit, in the unquiet sphere. *tell me
your dreams*, the sheer white veil, raised
slowly over my praying face. and the chorus of vows;
in sickness, in sickness I take you as my bridegroom.
your chest is buried, luminous, a sheet of perforated
wafers. and your blood flows carelessly, wine-purple on
my lips. my bouquet is brittle; femur, ulna,
vertebrae, and I throw it in the flames, the red
sleeves and bodices of the bridesmaids. your virgin
attendants and I, our sceptres shining, surround you

and pick at your flesh, tearing it with our teeth and
fingers. my mouth envelops your heart, and pulls it,
wet and beating, from its setting. delicious muscle,
raw, unseasoned. he interprets this, and other dreams
for me, unmoved. our therapy is a rosary, he said.
each violet jewel evokes him, the golden saviour at
the centre, and heals my night-terror, my *psychose
passionnelle.*

2

on the universal tendency to debasement in the sphere of love

it is common, he said, for patients to fall in love
with me. your desires secured in cardboard folders—
ciphers, cautious cryptograms. I am the man you
always wanted, my thoughts are a mystery to you.
and my gestures, the hand at my throat, the
speculum, are as remote as the distance between us.
the letters I leave him are erotomanic,
I ask him to bandage my chest in emerald gauze,
to apply leeches, annelidan silk, to my
palms. and to imagine me, breathless beneath his
delicate scalpel, each kiss sutures, stitches him
closer. each time I ask him, he frowns and deceives me.
and finally, he asks me to leave. he can't help
me, but I may call his archangelic name after
he is gone. he will be a parable, a bird, a mustard
seed. I will live in you, if you remember me,
I thought he understood. *my mind's not right,*
it breaks at the thought, remember. I am curious
as I array his body on the pile carpet

into new shapes, a paring knife, a hook, a bowl.
before breaking his putrid bones, before extinguishing
his appetite for beauty, before incanting the *Manifeste
Cannibale*. I exhaust my hunger, at the banquet
of his corpse. liver terrapin, kidney rosettes,
sweet spleen marinade. he was afraid, I think,
but in the shadows, the seaweed of my appetite,
he forgives me. and requites my love, patient, absolute,
as he slowly vanishes from sight.

๑ Strange Fits of Passion

for Xaviera Hollander

Strange fits of passion have I known:
And I will dare to tell,
But in the Lover's ear alone,
What once to me befel.
    —William Wordsworth

I lick my lover's ear and it burns
as my tongue traces the love,
helix, ossicula. his hands reach for
the ribbons, the snap-panel of my
edible underpants, he wants to
taste the sugar, its sweet fruit
centre. he moans as I slap his hands
away; as I unclasp my tiger-skin
bustier; my red ruffled garter and
I slide my stockings slowly
past my thighs knees and ankles.
I ask him to strip and gaze as he
peels away his vest, his nylon
socks, his mesh briefs and stands
nervous and hopeful, before me.
now dance, I say, in these manacles
and restraints. I sway my silver
hair to the mariachi songs
and the radio plays into the
hot evening and he turns and spins
and listens

this happened to me when I was
a madam and I never told a soul.

but I confessed everything else:
the baleful eyes of the german
shepherd that licked my thighs
and raked me with his saffron paws,
the boy whose come tasted like
clotted cream, the first girl I
ever kissed when I was a child
and her nipples were pastille-sweet
in my mouth. I was unbearably
beautiful then. the sky was my
replica, cheekbone steeples and
the silver mist of my pale
moonlit hair. I was making
breakfast for my girls, in a
gingham apron and bonnet.
poffertjes, little puff pancakes,
and *ontbijtkoek*. Helen was brushing
the pans with melted butter,
her fingers were shining translucent
and I saw the sun burn against the
depressions in the metal. I
reached out and touched the soft
wildflowers, the sleeves of her
nightgown. she held me in her
arms and we kissed below the
casement windows where the
glass panes shook and the tulip
bulbs trembled in their pots.
and all the saints came, with
pastry dolls and abject potato
parings wrapped in paper and string.
we cut them open and found the red
inlaid stones inside, we wore them
in our navels as we walked. slowly,

up the stairs, our clothes drifted
to the landing, our hands
bound with a delicate web. as
we ascended, I watched the sun drop
into the poplars and my heart
beat, faster, it constricted in my
chest. I turned to her and saw
her face, radiant in the light
as the cruel branches reached and
devoured the sun and I cried,
I screamed if Helen should be dead!
she murmurs quietly into the night
and bathes my face with cool water,
witch hazel. but I am inconsolable,
I stare at the stars and I understand.
for it is written there, I tell him,
all of it. there is my body, holy,
luminous and there is the space
the impression of Helen, of Helen lost
against me. her eyes were white and still,
her lips bled as we parted. the storm
clouds, the bruises on her battered face.
he resembled you, I said,
he had your desire.

he was quiet also, and I whipped him, I
ground my heels in his chest until
he begged for mercy.

☙ Poems for Jack the Ripper

1. He also serves who only stands and waits

and somehow you asked me to stay
but not to ask why
no not to ask why

I have never discovered your
identity, although we
were very close once.
there were several clues,
a scraping of skin, the
atlas of scars beneath
the tissue on my chest.
at the time, I asked you
about the others and you
said *what does it matter*
when you're the one I love?
you could be tender, pulling
me close when I screamed, and
in the orange of your nightgown
I was enveloped by the moon.
but sometimes I am afraid.
when the shadows fall, in long
slivers in the mist. and your feet
creep in the corners, in the black
edges of the night. a rustle,
of dead leaves and pale white bone.
you have returned, unknown, to
these narrow streets. my heart is
a bad neighbourhood, its tenements
lie derelict, condemned.

to remember you, to feel your
cold fingers closing my eyes,
once more.

she is almost a wraith, she is
not apparent. her green eyes
are luminous, the clockface
that glows as I lay awake,
turning. I have seen this colour
before, a sick jealous glare.
a thorn in my side when I asked
you, again and again, where you
were, the night before. your
surgical gloves run pink under
the tap, you look dishevelled
and wild. you said I was suspicious,
you said terrible things: *why
don't you kill yourself?* I had
let myself fall apart, and she,
she is frail and pitiless. her
hair is lace, wormwood and there
is bile flowing sweetly
from her lips.

I sensed that things were
not right, the crimson ink
blotted on mysterious envelopes,
the newspaper, sliced to ribbons.
I saw you dreamily folding
flour and kidney into a pie shell,
and you smiled. you looked
strangely beautiful as
you placed it before me.

I had written, urgently,
privately, *God help me*,
and I came to regret this.
your surveillance was exhaustive,
and I cried the night I burned my
letters. you made a mark on my
forehead with the ashes, you
left that night, and I waited
by the window, anxious,
contrite. when the light
broke through the shutters,
I heard you, heavy on the
stairs. I heard the bloodhounds
too, and the grieving sirens.
there was no sign of resistance,
she held her arms benevolently to
the bitter sky. I have no malice,
no wisdom to give her, because I
could not resist him. his
hate, his cruelty pulls like a stone,
and I fall, beneath the cold dark
water, of seduction.

2. I prayed in Whitechapel

I fell to the floor of the white
chapel, at the altar and it
was late October. the icy
wind rattled the clerestory
windows, where the chilly
sun bleaches his sorrowful
face. my god, is delinquent,

his eyes clamped shut. as
a procession of children,
dressed as witches, lizards,
quiet petunias, file solemnly
below. a girl, in white tulle,
touches my hand with a paper
star and I shake with nausea.
the tile floor is cool against
my cheek, I am dreaming. he is
carving pumpkins in the gaslight,
their dreadful smiles are uneven,
burning. he is listening to
Tosca, with the sound turned low:
Ecco vedi, e merce d'un tou detto,
I implore him, to speak to me.
the point of the knife shines
as it disappears, into the
pocket of his overcoat. his
shoes, his shirtsleeves are
pocked with brilliant red.
It's part of my costume, he
explains to me; *I am wearing
a disguise*. he pulls a stocking
over his face and stares through
its sliced foot-seam. *Don't
wait up, I will be quite late.*
the pumpkin bread is warm in
the oven, for his return.
my nails are coated with
the slippery rind, and I
bite them, nervously, as
I rise to leave.

3. Remorse

sometimes, when I am cleaning
the broken glass and splinters,
the gale of his temper. he
looks remorseful, he says:
I can't seem to help myself.
he would be reading in the basement—
Tales from the Crypt—and his father
would find him and beat him with
a leather belt, and burn the
horror comics in the backyard.
he remembers the weird green haze,
of the fire, watching their paper
faces, powerless, as the unkind orange
terror effaces them. he heard
his mother playing the organ, mournfully,
from a distance, *How Great Thou Art:*
he sees the stars, he hears
the roar of thunder, forever
in his temples, beating.
and he is still, after the anger passes.
I smooth the damp hair from his forehead,
and he clutches a faint rag doll
to his chest. he traces its mouth, a line
of yarn stitches and cries,
the tears fall like comets
on its button eyes. he says,
I wish all things were alive.

4. the miracle fish

she places the fortune teller
fish, a sliver of red cellophane,
on her palm. its tail turns over:
False, she is untrue to me. she
crumples it and it is motionless
when I touch it: *Dead One*. she
loves symmetry, deception,
her voice is the light rustle,
the bat whispers. her bed
is papered, with gift wrapping,
mash notes. I recognize his
signature, a cloak and dagger;
I look away. her silence
is beguiling, emerald grass,
the burnished earth of my
grave. I relinquish this
delirium, because I need courage.
to love her, although she is
also deadly, such thorns in
my skin. she asks for my blessing,
and receives it. passion flowers,
arrayed brightly on her wedding
gown. I am streaming petals
behind her as she walks,
each apostle glows in the violet
night. the air is sweet with
pollen and he is breathless,
when he looks beyond me,
at her glorious approach.

5. *Few are left unafraid of the phantom killer*

he left suddenly, and never returned,
but he is still out there.
I hear him, the cautious step,
the spin of the grindstone.
he was careful, meticulous;
he placed my rings and hair-
pins in a circle, as I slept.
my vanity, he said, a dubious
halo. the knife inches closer
to my neck, he is sallow,
malevolent. telling me to
die, *I hate the sight of you,*
walking the street. running,
down the street to escape him,
I fall down and he steps on my
arms and cuts me. *I'm not what*
you think, I tell him, choking
on blood, the panic. but it's
hopeless, he overcomes me.
a viridian wave. and slices
his name, deep, in my heart.
where it blisters and flames;
he kisses me, coldly—
I hear *Murder* in the echoes—
and he promises me, we will
meet again.

ᴏ The Chicken Baby

A car radio bleats,
"Love, O careless Love...." I hear
my ill-spirit sob in each blood cell
     —Robert Lowell

Jack and I were fighting—he threw
knives and flames over my head and they
sailed to the floor below us.
the fire began there, in the Ministry
of Love. because there were no windows,
he explained. and we were slow,
the glow of little sunsets: valium,
this was lovely and calm. yellow,
burning, his voice (calling me) was
always sweet. golden veins,
threading the intemperate earth;
I slashed at his arms, his ankles,
as we left; I renewed myself with
these riches.

he was a vision in sky-blue, and I
was converted. I saw *signs and wonders*
I did not believe. light, flowing
from the gas-elements. in the
cold night, the ants and silverfish
moved in careful circles and we
were quiet as the rain beat against
the ceiling glass. this was long before
he became remote and I became dangerous.
he worked, very briefly, as a sailor
and I slept with my hands in the waves.

I lay, like a message in the sand,
waiting for his safe return.

he turned away because his bones
ached, and I looked at the anatomy
of his accidents. shadows,
pain, in the interstices between
flesh and metal. he cries out in
his dreams, when I trouble these
spaces, when I push him, angrily,
hard. Helen, then, was my closest
friend. her beautiful face was notorious;
she had caused anguish, destruction.
I was aware of her senseless grace,
the swan-feathers that coronate her hair.
she is insidious, artless, her
eyes, her mouth a *moist mistake*.
but her small affections have left
me defenceless, as though my
faith is lattice-work, as though
he knows this, he sings:
the fault is not mine, not
mine

my hands burn in their bandages;
Helen is nervous and unsure when
she tells me she loves him.
I tell her that he is
no longer of this world. I
have gathered what remains,
a brown envelope: letters, ribbon,
ash, a sepia picture. he is alone,
gesturing, to the presents concealed

in his pockets. he was devoted to
arcane objects, *chinoiserie.* I
remember, with pain, the chicken-
baby. pink-felt sleeper, orange
eyes; he placed it in my palm,
its voice a passionate squeak—
Love, O careless Love.

nothing is ever demolished by
fire, or history. when I
returned home, after his
furious departure, like a bride,
like a queen, it lay beheaded.
pearls of stuffing, that led
to nothing; his absence is
palpable now. I have always
been lonely, he knew this and
more. that I would paste and
sew each piece together.
that I would recognize him,
his frail likeness, that flares
like a miracle in everything
that is broken, and lost.

ᔧ Ultra Violet

complaint by night of the lover not beloved

in Italy an artist proposes a shrine to Santa Ultra Violetta

I am wearing crystal-haze drop earrings, a
fake black Breitschwantz coat and pillbox
hat. I am holding a Bible in my hand.
marked with a paper cross at Colossians,
and this I say, lest any man should
beguile you. with false devotion, I recite
the *Recessional.* for my Madonna,
little Mary/Andy magnificat, my soul
does magnify him this night. his pearl
white hair and gimlet eyes, sun-black,
and cruel. I remember his cool skin, his
alchemy. he spilled diamond dust, silver
mercury on my shoes, he named me Notre Dame
when I kissed him. he is afraid of me,
he shrinks when I touch him. the base metal
of my Chanel chains is gold in his fingers,
a bright aurora, a polestar. I would meditate
to find my own name, beneath his purple-
orange daisies, the stalks of polished grass.
I divine within the words, I slice the page
with tantric scissors, *Ultra Violet.* my
cells split and bloom in incarnation, I recall
the *Sonnet des Voyelles.* five vowels, each
one a colour, the beet I press to my cheeks,
lemon juice, red grapes, purple broccoli.
the crushed cranberries in my tangled hair,
stuck with ostrich plumes, a plum velvet dress.

pansies arch my doorways, windowsill, *more and
more I identify with the violet.* I wear its
essence with rose geranium, patchouli, and study its
properties in the Complete Herbal: a dram
weight of its dried leaves in wine rids
the body of choleric humours, its
petals soothe insomnia and pleurisy. the
sorrows of adoration, the cold baby in a white
basin, its seedling arms and selfish lips.
I am someone else, not Isabelle, when I
walk the streets in peso-skirts and jewelled
slippers. if you could see my eyes then,
the militia of lashes, the ianthine rims.
and praise my beauty, in *billets doux:
Violette, la Catholique, je t'adore.*
even as my flesh became weak, the blood
coursing down my legs, *I feel so desperately
ill, I know I must be dying*, love me, I
prayed. I dreamed, many times, prophetically.
cardboard pyramids, glass beakers, an
X-ray machine that shrinks my spirit, *in excelsis.*
and finally, I dream a field of violets. I
bottle them, and cut them open. their colour,
seeds pour over my hands as I try
to push them together again. this vision
consoles me until you push me away,
I push you away, and I am lighter than air.
imagining, if I were an amethyst, I would
be peerless in each setting, in the
filigree of romance. the avarice,
the absolute thrill of discovery, I
think about this jewel as I leave the
cemetery. how it creates itself from

sediment and rock, how precious it is, how
well it wears its years of obscurity.
I write this to tell the living,
you possess the earth, its stillness
and solitude, but the rest, my beloved,
is mine.

❧ Skirt, My Pretty Name

and the space between my name and myself grows larger until...
    —Rosalie Sings Alone

after several valium and a cup of coffee, I
    feel sweet and contented. the city is dangerous,
prurient and I am a woman of mystery. I ask
    the waitress for some napkins and whisper,
my husband's brains are in my hands. I ask her
    to regard the blood and tissue, the horror of my
dress. I am wearing tinted sunglasses, a chiffon
    scarf, patterned with lemons and cherries.
my wig, my hair is concealed, it really is
    awful, a cerise-coloured rat's nest and it itches,
badly. when I leave, I move smoothly through the streets,
    clutching my shopping bags; I fit my key into
the lock and gaze at my calling card, that reads:
    skirt, my pretty name

I am applying lee press-on nails and listening to
    The Magic of Mantovani. I am having a nervous
breakdown. *you don't bring me flowers*, I remember
    coming home once and finding a sprig of lilacs
on my doorstep and I held them and *I thought of him*
    I love. he was a merchant marine, and I was his
noviciate. I held conch shells to his ears
    while he slept, so he could hear the sea,
the sheets billowed like sails when he kissed
    me. he would powder my nose, he traced his
fingers down my thighs, *my flaw.* he was never,
    he was rarely cruel to me. when he left, I
wore a mourning veil and sewed starfish over my
    eyes. I cried like a siren, I slashed my

wrists with a broken bottle. it lay on the carpet
    shattered, with a message, a silver ship in
its base

weeks in the hospital, without perfume, or candy,
    and I still have no friends. yesterday, a man
came over to me and screamed about the accident, the
    blood! I shrank, smaller, into my sweater
and imagined I was somewhere else. the women in the
    restaurant smile when I take their pictures
with a pink instamatic and I offer them spoonfuls of
    chocolate, my number. I am staring at the
telephone now, willing it to ring, cradling it in my
    arms and my stomach is turning. I beat myself
with my fists, I stick my ribs with pins and
    needles, my loneliness is relentless. I see
its constancy in the spreading bruises, the green
    and yellow echoes. I am the quietest object here,
I could rest here always, never moving

only breathing, the faintest shadow. slowly
    turning the pages of my library book:
Fashion in the 1970's and naming the dances
    under my breath. I would step from
side to side and do the hustle, but I am
    tired and solemn. I am the light that
jewels their white pantsuits; the mirrored
    disco-ball made of shattered stars.
the dancers sway beneath me in an orbit and
    sometimes stare, with a comb or a
tissue. they see that they are broken,
    mortal, and they look away.

❧ Dracula Has Risen From the Grave

for Alice

And what, if in a world of sin
(O sorrow and shame should this be true!)...
    —Samuel Taylor Coleridge, "Christabel"

I shiver when the sun sinks behind the lowering clouds,
and pull on the batwing sleeves of my tiny dress.
there are green mists, rising like strange vines from
the sewer grates; I see the car, its dull headlights
approaching—it slows to a crawl beside me.
I beckon to him, and he motions me inside, his long
yellow fingernails pulling a sheaf of bills across the
plush velvet upholstery. there are brass handles on the
door, and heaps of earth potted on the purple floor.
where it is written: *For the Blood Is the Life.*
it is like a coffin in here, the song on the radio is
funereal, *how sweet the sound.* of forgetfulness,
the plain, painful memory of Mina, lilies crossed on
her quiet breast, her unearthly pallor.

she would stand on the street corner like a queen,
her white hair combed into an elaborate pompadour.
I touched the soft beauty-mark on her cheek, the
satin ribbons that curled against her neck. like
crimson bites; I buried my mouth in her shoulders,
her throat and felt the sweet, certain beat of her heart.
she showed me pictures in books of places we would
visit. I would sleep, in the cold mornings, dreaming
of her, following her through stone courtyards,
into the dark green sea. I gave her ermine slippers,

44

silk wrappers and scarves, but her breath was visible,
her skin turned slowly blue. she told me about a man who
had tried to seduce her, even after she was finished. he pushed
his tongue into her ears, he bit her lips until they bled.
he said he could be anything, any shape he chose and she
heard the call of wolves, wild and binding. she heard him answer
and her chest ached, she began to shake, from fever and distress.
her struggle quickened his movements, he seemed to flourish—
her illness was brief and she died alone, resting on a wooden chair,
before the narrow window. I could not bear to think of her body,
her voice consoling me, because I was unloved,
because she

reached out, with trembling arms. her hands spread out, her
eyes clenched shut: she had a horror of the sun. I watched her
until it set and I dressed to leave, my face set with *dull and
treacherous hate*. I knew he would come for me, that I would
see his rear-view mirror, that he would not be reflected there.
he compels me to behold him, to see him in his splendour.
the decadent prince I can not refuse; as I offer him my wrists,
my neck, my eyes are red and fierce. he devours them and I pray
for Mina, I pray she is undead. undead, as I lose the light,
the air, without resistance, or remorse.

☙ I Am Curious (Yellow)

And yet I was not unhappy, for I lived entirely for love.
   —Jane DeLynn

he is such a slut, he tells me he never
wears underwear. he gestures, between his legs
and I think of the cool air, arousing him.
there is ice on the streets, ice like glass and I
fell, (*Oh God, I fell for you*). I brought
him a pot of tulips, pink, tender, barely
blooming. he is unconscious of metaphor,
my desire is parenthetical, unseen.
as if I am undercover (purple satin sheets
that cling to his thighs), I listen for
clues when he speaks. I decipher his kiss:
the bitter taste—small green apples—
his mouth is insistent, and I am breathless,
curious. yellow light filters through the
keyhole, he closes the door (*green
with silver hinges*) behind me, suddenly.
I am left alone with my thoughts of love,
my undeviating fictions.

his little rejections are stimulating; he
compounds what is mysterious, what is unknown:
he is *a man loved wholly beyond wisdom*,
half sick of shadows, I compel myself
to see him, to see him for the first time.
there are amber scales on his crooked teeth;
once, I thought of golden scarabs, pressed
gold leaf. once, he told me he enjoyed
hurting me, *I live for it*, he said.

I thought I was dead, I envied him that much.
with my head buried in my collar, slowly,
I begin to *undress him with my eyes*.
each grey scrap—a worry bead—his sad strip-
tease bewitches me. his pale flesh begins to
emerge, his spine, a fleet silhouette, a lizard,
distressed. he is mortified, as he reveals himself,
beneath the gale winds, the cruel force
of my predatory gaze.

there are seedlings in the snow, fragile
green shoots. that are tulips, that will be tulips,
as the sun assists them in their ascent.

I think of the way tulips look when they die; the petals
unfold and surrender their centre to the sun.

how the barren seeds cling faintly to the obdurate heart,
and perish, as they come undone.

ᴄ Little Stabs At Happiness

If I'm too rough, tell me
I'm so scared
Your little head will come off
with my hands
    —Alice Cooper

every angel is terrible, and the one
I love is sly, inscrutable.
there are lines on his face
that foretell my portion,
and silently I behold him.
you are the one, he tells me,
as I twist together: carbon,
radio wire, a beam of light.
midnight blue, the colour of
his eyes. I have patented
my own invention. a shrinking-
ray gun and I have brought it here
for you. he doesn't stir, even
as I place the barrel next to
his temple and compress. his molecules
glow like little stars and diminish.
and I fold him into a tissue and muffle
his screams.

I hear my father's nervous foot-
steps on the stairs. my convex
pocket, the squeaks, unnerve him.
behind the door, I slowly unwrap
him, my flame. he is white and
still and I hold him to my mouth

and give him *the kiss of life*.
he blinks and shudders and I remove
his garments, the miniature
socks and cotton briefs. and lay him,
trembling against my heart.
its ventricles open and close
like church doors, my blood is
hot and sentient beneath him.
my fingers explore his
neck, his chest, the soft space
between his shoulders
and I weep, silently, because he
is my first lover, and because
it hurts to touch him.

once, it was enough to stare
at him: my ceiling is
celestial with his image.
I painted his face on my
pillow and held him to me,
until I choked. and the letters
I sent were always the
same, pink clouds, ardently
perfumed and stiff with rejection.
soon I developed a longing,
a taste for him I could not
requite. his skin is the
salt, sweet bliss I imagined.
I am sorry he struggles,
when I hold him, when we
tumble into bed and he strains
until a pattern of diamonds is
raised on his back. once,

he seemed as infinite as space,
a forbidden planet, he is
palpable now. I hear the sirens
in the distance, I hear:
abduction. a cruel word that
does not describe my *adoration*.
and I know I must divest myself of him,
one last time, my deshabille.
I clean him with cotton and alcohol
and preserve him. each stroke, each
little stab at happiness will depress
him. he is the culture, the essence of the
medicine, the antidote I have
devised. to remedy the pain,
the violence of love; its formula
glows in my darkened bedroom as the red
lights begin to sweep steadily
over the street, the trees.

❧ Painting With Elke Sommer

Oh, I'll content him,—but to-morrow, Love!
I often am much wearier than you think
    —Andrea del Sarto

here is one of my earliest paintings:
a white cat, a bowl of zinnias, a speckled eggshell.
the lines are precise and well defined—I began
as an illustrator for my husband's salon.
I designed the napkins and matchbooks:
Coiffures à la mode pour hommes. three
stylish profiles with pompadours and
geometrical sideburns [*in triangle inequalities,*
the sum of two sides of a triangle is greater than
the third side]. during my apprenticeship,
he would reach for me, but I was tired, distracted,
working with a slide rule and compass, perfecting my
art. I made plaster casts, colour charts (from
pale blue to violet), I folded paper into
artichokes and drapery. he was ardent, insistent,
he left bouquets of condoms—ribbed and glowing—
in water jars, he lay naked on my worktable.
arrayed in sheets like a Roman soldier as
I painted the folds of linen, his discontent.
and soon he stopped coming home at all. he fell in
love with a stylist, who tinted his hair every night—
a rainbow—and he sang to me, *Cherish,* he sang this under
my window occasionally: *perish is the word that*
more than applies. he was a troubadour and I was grinding
pigments, stretching my canvas into circles and flowers.
I painted camels and topless dancers, I rendered
the evening sky, and I imagined I was the spirit,

the motion at the centre. my blonde hair grew
silver roots and I baked in the sun like an urn,
like a grecian urn.

my attic shape, my ravished skin, I see the symbols,
Instruments of the Passion, when I stare into the
mirror. I think love was never so simple, as the
yards of black velvet, the pristine edge of my
palette knife. I am working on a series of self-portraits,
modelled on my days in the cinema. seductive,
desirable, I am painted in spangles, I receive the
gaze of the matador, and hold eternity, a fig-leaf, a
bunch of grapes, in my fingers. but *the subject/object
is abject* and I come to despise her, the dead woman.
so I languish until I sleep and it comes to me,
the annunciation. and I paint portrait after portrait
of big-eye Elkes; the resemblance is perfect,
but the eyes are colossal. they are pools
of tranquillity, they reduplicate my soul.
and in their corners, a few tears well and glisten,
my artist's heart is fragile, and I am
grateful, dearest God, for this blessing.

✺ Corporal Punishment

A cleft in your chin instead of your foot
But no less a devil for that, no not
    —Sylvia Plath

I am troubled by his nightstick, his baton.
as if he were pressing it against my thighs,
as if his handcuffs snaked slowly around
my ankles. his cropped hair is a
bed of sweetgrass and his holster drops,
in a clatter. a leather shadow, burning
at the foot of the bed. when he cruises
by me in the late afternoon, I think he
may arrest me, this time, or maybe soon.
somewhere, at a dance club, he will
sidle up to the bar, slowly, and offer me
money. when I reach for the flower of
green and blue bills, he will pull out his
badge. I will fix my lipstick in its
bright reflection and offer him my hands.
I have dressed carefully in garters, seamed
stockings, a rayon wig. *you bastard*, I
say, tenderly, as he leads me to the back seat
of the car. the seat where the windows and
doors won't open, it is a dream, I am
floating in space, I am dying. in the
compass, the space where his thumbprints
bruise my wrists. *my darling*, I breathe
into the inkpad, the camera. *will you keep*
this on your dresser, querida? and look at
me, when you prick your fingers, sewing
your medals to your white shoulders. you

will tremble as the blood wells and hold me
closer, even closer

my father was a car thief, I remember
the wire hangers in his suit pocket, the
hot wires. he would sit and tattoo his
chest and stomach with food dye and a safety pin.
pale red spark-plugs, a pair of dice;
he told me about the long arm of the law.
touching my hair, through the branches
of the trees that framed my window.
combing it into a shining French roll.
in Paris, I walk with the corporal, in a grey
and white striped *chemise*. he slaps me when he
learns I have been unfaithful and we drink
cassis—the blood of black currants, heavy and
sweet. I take his pearl-handled revolver,
for target practice. the tin cans on the fence,
lychees in syrup, are ragged with holes and flowing
as I fire. and fire, the polished metal of his
abdomen is brazen in the flames and his tongue
splits as he calls my name,
Miranda, and I shudder.

I embrace the pillows and sheets,
alone on my bed I reduce him. my
lover is the interval, inside the
gun barrel. he is the bore, the
emptiness I devour, when I am
hungry and in the mood for love.

➸ Jesus the Low Rider

take a little trip
take a little trip with me

I see him through the keyhole,
swaying below the porchlight and his halo of moths.
I smell the wine on his breath and I feel
weak in the knees: *this is my blood*.
I release the chain and fall into his arms,
again. *his cheeks are comely with rows of*
jewels, his neck with chains of gold.
he wears an iron cross, a confederate
bandanna and his chain-whips clamour,
they sting my fingers when I undress him.
the soles of his motorcycle boots are
the cartography of his absences, each run,
each time he leaves I swear it is the last time.
as the door slams and I sweep the glass and
splinters, his temper is epic and desperate:
I love an outlaw

who talks about betrayal in his sleep,
his hands rake the sheets and I cleanse
them, *with tears*. in the morning
I hear the Apostles circling, their
high-raked mufflers are stormclouds
that portend my loss, my loneliness.
Christ, I am desolate without him.
he bakes loaves of bread in high
spirits and I remove the oilcoth—
my shroud of Turin—and polish the
bike. its suicide clutch and chrome rails

shine with water and vinegar, there
is a prophetic grammar in their
dagger-design. I see the crash that
kills him, the rain-soaked road,
his stillness. I see myself
in shadow, resurrecting him. I
have the gospel lettered on my
forearms, in gold and green.
I have learned to live with sorrow,
and I am a believer. Jesus kisses
me, hard on each cheek, before he
turns, and rides away.

ᔕ **He Scares Me So**

I never thought I'd come to this...

my outfit, discarded on a chair, is a conversion
narrative. a tunic, imprinted with the Seven Seals,
a rayon shirt that depicts the moon landing. intrepid
astronauts, placing little flags in violet craters.
I had rarely thought of Him—since my confirmation,
but I remember the impression of His head, on the pillow
beside me. protecting me; I erase this image from my
face with pancake makeup, and see another image there. *my*
cheeks are all eaten with makeup, I am almost feverish.
as I drift through the silent streets to the first
performance of Jesus Christ Superstar.

I am mad to oppose the stars, I see the bones of lost
friends, pure white, singing. there are angels in the snow,
with coal black eyes, and flowing skirts. the psychedelic
glow—blue sunshine—in my veins, my heart. I am
alone, anonymous when I watch the opera, wild with
sympathy. for Mary, *she has had so many men before;*
in very many ways, He's just one more. I have also loved
the likes of Him, mysterious, distracted, His quickening
rage. He is screaming in the temple in a divine temper and
she consoles Him, *myrrh for His hot forehead, O.* I am
suddenly tired of consolation: I *understand what power is,*
understand what glory is.

it is, this time, the hulking figure of the Centurion.
who averts his eyes and scourges Christ, he silences
Him (he brings Him to His knees) with a foot on His hem
and the vinegar, the tears are burning on my cheeks.

he is desirable to me even later, as he presses through
the crowd from the stage and I move quietly behind him. I slip
my hand beneath his leather waistband and touch the small
of his back. *I want what you have*, I tell him,
in a perilous voice. he misunderstands, and turns
and crushes me in his arms. he mashes his lips to
mine and I feel his mouth open, his tongue depresses
mine in one swift gesture. I rake my nails down
his neck until he cries out, furious. as I walk home,
I suck his blood from my fingers, and wonder why he
ruined everything; I think of gravity

annihilating the sky. that evanesces above me,
there are pieces missing from my life, I know this.
and still, I am confounded by science, the laws of
attraction. the apparent brightness of a star
depends on two things: *how much light it radiates...*
and how far it is, how far it is from me.

✑ Nancy Drew's Theatre of Blood

the truth loves me
—Sylvia Plath

the proprietor of Salome's is a
fallen man. unloved, anxious, but
he smiles at me as I enter.
the pink walls are a mardi gras
of whips, chain mail and leatherette.
an apothecary of lotions, botanical
green condoms in red-petal foil.
the spiked dog collars, the manacles
seduce me: *Call in my death's-head
there; tie up my fears.* but I want
something playful, a mask with
oblong cat's eyes, a tasselled
merry widow. I select emotion—
lotion and find it spreads like
ice, and then burns—like revenant
fury—under my tongue.
   my father leaves out details of
    her death, *a crossword cipher.* she
     was very unhappy, she often slept for
      hours in the afternoon. the rope,
       the noose is a ghost in the prisms of
      the chandelier, her footprints a
      fresco on the papered walls. the shattered
      jar on the parquet floor, laudanum,
      vaseline. her blue negligee: an·
     apparition.

because he is a lawyer, he defends her.
pleasure eluded her; she

reached to the hot centre of
the sky, she tormented fate. she knew
the danger and rarely resisted. he leaves me
a pamphlet entitled *Autoerotic
Hanging*. he encourages me to leave
her flowers, prayers, by the toppled
chair, it is her cenotaph and it remains
there.

but she remains close, she seems to
hold me in her arms and squeeze. she
is a sleek and dangerous python, who
batters my senses. she sings, a burlesque
song of love. I detect a tremor in her voice,
you must be careful darling. there is a warp,
an imperfection

in the lens of my spyglass, that dangles
over the field of black and white
squares, the midriff of my dress.
when the queen has been sacrificed, the
king is in danger. he moves slowly to
the centre. and the bishop glides to
meet him; she is radiant in a starched
white apron, a three-cornered hat.
she hands me heart-shaped cookies,
fresh from the oven. and scrapes at Carson's
shirtsleeves with salt and soda water
until the kiss (the feverish stain on
his neck and breastbone) disappears.

Hannah often vanishing as my mother's
plaintive voice called from the bedroom.
quickly smoothing her hair, her sash

and the rosewater of her flushed face.
she cried at the funeral, and I watched
tissue after tissue fall into her
crocodile purse.

was his hand warm, urgent on her
thigh, is she still tender, still
silent?

their stolen moments, their ardor is
X-rated, erotic to me. even as I reconstruct
the murder, their assignations excite my
fancy and I cherish them.
I am becoming more and more perverse.
 I want to join them some day, when the
  lights are low. slipping into something
   more comfortable, the discipline
    number. *you are your mother's daughter*,
    he says. but the structure of S/M is
   fluid and changing. and it is the dominatrix
  who binds their faithless hands
together: exacting punishment.

I am all that remains of her;
detection also made her sick.
but the urge to recover is less
compelling than the thrall, the
passion of the truth that loves me.

Editor for the Press: Christopher Dewdney
Cover Design: Pippa White
Author Photograph: Alice Palumbo
Printed in Canada

Coach House Press
50 Prince Arthur Avenue, Suite 107
Toronto, Canada M5R 1B5